THE ART OF NETWORKING

Unlock the Power of Connection for Career and Business Success

Ray Goodwin

CONTENTS

Title Page

Copyright

LIABILITY DISCLAIMER

The information contained within this book is intended for informational purposes only and should not be construed as legal or professional advice. The authors and publishers of this book are not responsible for any losses or damages that may arise from the use of the information contained within.

The reader assumes full responsibility for any decisions made based on the information in this book. The authors and publishers do not endorse any particular method, service or product mentioned in this book and are not responsible for any consequences resulting from their use.

The reader should exercise caution and discretion when making life changing decisions, and should be aware of the risks and potential consequences of their actions. This book is not a substitute for professional or legal advice and should not be relied upon as such.

By reading and using the information in this book, the reader acknowledges and agrees to hold harmless the authors, publishers, and any other parties involved in the creation or distribution of this book from any and all liability, claims, damages, or losses that may arise from their use of the information contained herein.

CHAPTER 1: INTRODUCTION TO NETWORKING

Welcome to The Art of Networking, a practical guide to mastering the art of building professional relationships. In today's fast-paced and ever-changing world, networking has become a crucial skill for success in any field. Whether you are an entrepreneur, a freelancer, a job seeker or simply looking to expand your circle of peers, this book will provide you with the tools and strategies you need to develop meaningful connections that can help take your career to the next level.

As someone who has been involved in online sales for over 25 years, I have seen firsthand the power of networking when it comes to generating leads, closing deals and growing businesses. Through trial and error, I have learned what works and what doesn't when it comes to building relationships that last. In these pages, I will share with you my insights on how to network effectively both online and offline.

The Art of Networking is not just another how-to book on networking; it is a comprehensive guide that covers everything from identifying your goals and target audience to crafting an elevator pitch and following up after a meeting. This book will teach you how to approach networking as an opportunity to give rather than just receive. It will also delve into the psychological principles that underlie successful networking interactions.

Through practical tips, real-life examples and interactive exercises, The Art of Networking will equip you with the knowledge and confidence you need to build fruitful professional relationships that can open doors and propel your career forward.

Overview

Networking is often described as making genuine connections with people who share similar interests and goals. In business development, networking is a critical skill that can help individuals achieve their professional and personal goals and attain success.

The Importance of Networking in Various Fields

Networking is a crucial aspect of success in various fields, including entrepreneurship, sales, social impact, career advancement, and transitions. It is essential to have a robust network that can open doors to new opportunities, provide access to potential customers or clients, and offer crucial support during a career or personal crisis.

Networking is also crucial for individuals seeking mentorship, advice, and guidance from experienced professionals in their field. A strong network can provide access to people in leadership positions who can guide you in your career trajectory.

How Networking Can Help in Personal and Professional Growth

Networking can expand personal and professional growth opportunities by helping individuals make connections that can lead to new projects or job opportunities. A well-connected network can also offer various resources, such as advice and access to educational and training opportunities that can lead to personal and professional development.

Common Misconceptions About Networking

Networking misconceptions include the idea that it is only for extroverts; however, networking is essential for everyone and can be learned by anyone. There is also a misconception that networking events are merely opportunities for self-promotion rather than forming genuine connections. However, networking involves building strong relationships with people based on mutual trust and respect, which can lead to opportunities in the future.

Different Types of Networking

Networking can happen in various forms, such as attending industry events, meeting new people through friends, joining professional associations, or even online. Online networking includes engaging with people on social media, participating in online networking communities or discussion forums, and reaching out to people through direct messages.

How to Overcome Fear of Networking

For many people, networking can cause anxiety and fear. Often, people feel nervous when they are around strangers or in new situations. However, overcoming fear and anxiety requires preparation and practice. It is crucial to prepare a few open-ended questions before attending the networking event. This can help kick off the conversation and make it easier to interact with people.

Tools and Resources for Networking

Networking can involve various resources and tools, such as business cards, online profiles, and websites. A well-designed website and social media profiles can offer instant credibility and help potential connections connect with you quickly. Other resources that can be helpful in networking include relationship management software, CRM, or automation tools.

Setting Networking Goals

Setting networking goals can help individuals focus their networking to achieve specific goals. This can include identifying the types of people, events, or organizations that can help achieve those goals. By outlining achievable objectives, individuals can establish a plan and track progress as they navigate networking events successfully.

In conclusion, networking is a critical skill for personal and professional growth. Developing a robust network can lead to new opportunities, educational and training opportunities, mentorship, guidance, and even lifelong friendships. By overcoming misconceptions and fears, individuals can learn to network successfully. A solid network can lead to success in various fields, including entrepreneurship, sales, social impact, career advancement, and transitions. In the following chapters, we will explore how to set and achieve networking goals, build personal and corporate brands, and use social media and virtual tools for networking effectively.

CHAPTER 2:
BUILDING YOUR
PERSONAL BRAND

In today's rapidly changing business landscape, building a personal brand is essential to succeed in networking. Having a personal brand can help professionals and entrepreneurs stand out in a crowded market and create stronger connections with their target audience.

What is Personal Branding and Why it Matters?

Personal branding is the process of creating a unique identity, reputation, and image for an individual. It involves identifying and promoting strengths, values, and skills that differentiate a person from others in their field. Personal branding is not just for entrepreneurs; it's also for job seekers, career changers, and professionals who want to advance their career.

Building a strong personal brand is important for several reasons:

❖ To stand out in a crowded market: In today's competitive business world, it's hard to get noticed without a strong personal brand. Creating a unique identity that reflects your values, skills, and experience can help you stand out from the crowd and increase your visibility.

❖ To establish credibility and trust: A strong personal brand can establish credibility and trust with your audience. By showcasing your strengths, experience and achievements, you can build a reputation as an expert in your field.

❖ To attract opportunities: A personal brand can open up new opportunities, whether it's a new job, a business partnership, or a speaking engagement. It can also attract more clients and customers by demonstrating your unique value proposition.

Assessing Your Strengths and Weaknesses

Before building your personal brand, it's important to assess your strengths and weaknesses to identify what sets you apart from others in your field. Understanding your unique combination of skills and experiences can help you create a personal brand that reflects your strengths and values.

One way to assess your strengths and weaknesses is to conduct a SWOT analysis. SWOT stands for strengths, weaknesses, opportunities, and threats. A SWOT analysis can help you identify internal strengths and weaknesses and external opportunities and threats.

Identifying Your Unique Value Proposition

Your unique value proposition is what sets you apart from others in your field. It's a statement that explains the unique benefits of working with you.

To identify your unique value proposition, answer the following questions:

❖ What problems do you solve for your clients or customers?

❖ What benefits do your clients or customers receive from working with you?

❖ What makes your approach to solving problems unique?

❖ What skills or experiences do you have that others don't?

Defining Your Target Audience

Once you have identified your unique value proposition, it's important to define your target audience. Your target audience is the group of people you want to connect and build relationships with.

To define your target audience, answer the following questions:

❖ Who are your ideal customers or clients?

❖ What are their needs, pain points, and challenges?

❖ What motivates them to make a purchase or start a business relationship?

❖ Where do they spend time online and offline?

Creating a Compelling Elevator Pitch

An elevator pitch is a brief summary of who you are, what you do, and what you can offer your target audience. It's called an elevator pitch because it should be short enough to deliver in the time it takes to ride an elevator (less than 30 seconds).

To create a compelling elevator pitch, follow these tips:

❖ Start with a hook that captures your audience's attention.

❖ Mention your unique value proposition.

❖ Highlight your achievements, skills, or experiences that demonstrate your expertise.

❖ Make it relevant to your target audience.

❖ End with a call to action or next step.

Choosing the Right Communication Channels

In today's digital age, it's essential to choose the right communication channels to reach your target audience. Your communication channels should align with your unique value proposition and target audience.

Some communication channels to consider are:

❖ LinkedIn: LinkedIn is a professional networking platform that allows you to connect and build relationships with other professionals in your field.

❖ Twitter: Twitter is a micro-blogging platform that allows you to share short messages, interact with other users, and participate in industry conversations.

❖ Instagram: Instagram is a visual platform that allows you to showcase your brand visually through images or videos.

❖ Blogging: A blog is a great way to demonstrate your expertise and share valuable content with your target audience.

Developing a Consistent Visual Identity

Consistency is key when it comes to branding. A consistent visual identity can help build trust and recognition with your target audience.

Developing a visual brand identity involves choosing colors, fonts, and imagery that align with your personal brand and audience. Your visual identity should be consistent across all your communication channels, including your website, social media, and business cards.

Monitoring and Maintaining Your Online Reputation

Building a personal brand is not only about creating a positive image but also about managing your online reputation. A negative review or comment can damage your online reputation and credibility.

It's important to monitor your online reputation regularly and respond to any negative comments or reviews promptly. You can use online tools like Google Alerts, Hootsuite, or Brandwatch to monitor your online reputation and social media mentions.

To maintain a positive online reputation, follow these tips:

- ❖ Be authentic and transparent in your communication.
- ❖ Share valuable content, insights, and expertise.
- ❖ Engage with your audience and respond promptly to their questions and comments.
- ❖ Avoid controversial or offensive topics.
- ❖ Act professionally in all your interactions.

Conclusion

Your personal brand is a critical element of networking success. To build a strong personal brand, you need to assess your strengths and weaknesses, identify your unique value proposition, define your target audience, create a compelling elevator pitch, choose the right communication channels, develop a consistent visual identity, and monitor and maintain your online reputation. By building a memorable and trustworthy personal brand, you can increase your visibility, attract opportunities, and build stronger relationships with your target audience.

CHAPTER 3: SETTING NETWORKING GOALS

The effectiveness of networking hinges on the clarity of your objectives. Without solid goals in place, your networking efforts can quickly become aimless and unfocused. Setting networking goals is essential to ensure that your efforts align with your personal and professional aspirations.

Defining Your Purpose for Networking

Before establishing your networking goals, you should have a clear understanding of your purpose for networking. Are you looking to advance your career, build your business, or build relationships with like-minded individuals? Once you have identified your purpose, you can align your networking goals accordingly.

Setting SMART Goals

The next step in setting networking goals is to create specific, measurable, achievable, relevant, and time-bound (SMART) objectives. SMART goals help you to align your networking efforts with a measurable outcome.

For instance, if your goal is to build your business, your SMART objective could be to acquire 10 new clients within the next three months, and you will achieve this objective by attending three industry conferences and reaching out to your existing network for referrals.

Identifying Your Desired Outcomes

Your networking goals should also have a clear outcome in mind. Your desired outcome could be to acquire new business connections, strengthen existing relationships, or increase your visibility within your industry. Identify precisely what you hope to achieve through networking efforts, and work backwards to determine the steps you need to take to achieve those outcomes.

Determining the Right Events and Groups to Attend

Not all networking events or groups are created equal. To achieve your networking goals, it is essential to identify the events and groups that align with your objectives. Ask yourself, who are the people or organizations that I need to connect with to achieve my goals? Research and attend events where you are likely to meet people that can help you achieve your networking goals.

Creating a Networking Plan

Once you have identified your networking goals and desired outcomes, the next step is to create a networking plan. A networking plan helps you to prioritize your networking efforts, set realistic timelines, and hold yourself accountable for achieving your networking goals.

Your networking plan should include the specific actions you need to take to achieve your goals, such as attending industry events, participating in online groups, and reaching out to existing connections. It is also essential to include deadlines and metrics to track your progress towards your networking objectives.

Tracking and Evaluating Progress

Networking is an ongoing process, and monitoring your progress is key to determining your effectiveness. Regularly measuring the success of your networking efforts will help you to identify what's working and what's not, allowing you to adjust your networking plan, if necessary.

Your progress towards your networking goals can be measured by the number of new connections you've made, the number of referrals received, or new business acquired, or any other metrics relevant to your networking goals.

Adjusting Goals as Needed

Finally, as you continue to network, you may realize that your initial networking goals no longer align with your current objectives. Adjusting your goals is essential to ensure that your networking efforts remain relevant to your personal and professional growth.

Celebrating Successes

Networking goals take time and effort to achieve. Celebrating your successes, no matter how small, is key to staying motivated and acknowledging your progress. Celebrating your successes also helps to reinforce your networking efforts and provides you with the confidence to continue to move forward.

In Summary

Setting networking goals is essential to ensure that you're maximizing your networking efforts. Define your purpose for networking, set SMART objectives, identify your desired outcomes, determine the right events and groups to attend, create a networking plan, track and evaluate progress, adjust goals as needed, and always celebrate your successes.

CHAPTER 4: APPROACHING NETWORKING EVENTS

Networking events can be intimidating for many people. They may make you nervous, anxious, or uncomfortable, but there is no need to worry. Approaching networking events can be learned, and with practice, can become much more comfortable, even enjoyable.

Overcoming nerves and anxiety

The first step to approaching networking events is to address any nerves or anxiety you may have. This is normal, and many people feel the same way. First, take some time to prepare yourself mentally. Visualize a successful event where you meet new people, make connections, and learn new things. Take a few deep breaths and remind yourself that networking is an opportunity to learn, grow, and expand your professional and personal circles.

Tips for effective body language

Body language is crucial when approaching networking events. Good body language can signal to others that you are approachable, confident, and interested in what they have to say. Here are some tips to help you improve your body language:

- ❖ Stand tall and straight

- ❖ Open your arms and keep them uncrossed

- ❖ Maintain eye contact

- ❖ Smile genuinely and warmly

- ❖ Face the person you are speaking to

Starting conversations with strangers

One of the most challenging parts of approaching networking events is starting conversations with strangers. Here are some tips for initiating conversations:

- ❖ Approach someone who is alone or in a small group

- ❖ Introduce yourself with a handshake

- ❖ Ask open-ended questions, such as "What brings you here today?" or "What do you do for work?"

- ❖ Listen actively to their responses and ask follow-up questions

- ❖ Share your experiences and interests

- ❖ Find common ground to build a connection

Asking open-ended questions

Open-ended questions are questions that require more than a yes or no response. They encourage the other person to share more about themselves and can start a more meaningful conversation. Here are some examples:

- ❖ What inspired you to pursue your career?

❖ What are some of the biggest challenges you face in your work?

❖ What do you enjoy most about your job?

Listening actively

Listening actively is just as important as asking questions. Active listening means paying attention to what the other person is saying and demonstrating that you are engaged in the conversation. Here are some tips for active listening:

❖ Make eye contact

❖ Nod your head

❖ Ask follow-up questions

❖ Summarize what the other person has told you

❖ Show empathy for their experiences

❖ Avoid interrupting or dominating the conversation

Finding common ground

Finding common ground is essential for building connections at networking events. When you find something in common with someone, you create a basis for a relationship and can build from there. Here are some ways to find common ground:

❖ Ask about their hobbies or interests

❖ Discuss common experiences or challenges

❖ Share your experiences and interests

❖ Look for commonalities in your work or field

❖ Ask what they are passionate about

Exiting conversations gracefully

Exiting conversations can be awkward, but it's necessary to move on and meet new people. Here are some tips for exiting conversations gracefully:

- ❖ Thank the person for their time and conversation
- ❖ Mention something memorable about the conversation
- ❖ Exchange contact information if appropriate
- ❖ Explain that you would like to meet more people
- ❖ Offer to connect with them later

Following up after events

Following up after events is essential for continuing and expanding connections made at networking events. Here are some tips for following up:

- ❖ Send an email or LinkedIn message within 24-48 hours
- ❖ Reference something memorable from your conversation
- ❖ Offer to meet for coffee or a phone call
- ❖ Mention how you can be helpful to them
- ❖ Keep the relationship going with regular check-ins and updates.

By implementing these tips, attending networking events will become a less daunting prospect. Networking can be a fun and exciting way to meet new people, learn from those in other industries or with different experiences, and build lasting and meaningful relationships. Remember to focus on finding common ground and actively listening and engaging in conversations. Exiting gracefully and following up with new contacts are also vital aspects of successful networking. With time and practice, networking events will become just another part of your routine for personal and professional growth.

CHAPTER 5: BUILDING RELATIONSHIPS

Networking is all about building relationships. However, it is not just about adding new contacts in your network; it's more about cultivating genuine connections and nurturing them over time. In this chapter, we will explore the value of building solid relationships through networking and learn how to develop them.

The Importance of Building Relationships

Building relationships is at the core of effective networking. People do business with people they know, like, and trust. Investing time and effort into developing meaningful relationships is a crucial step in building long-term success in any field.

In any fruitful connection, trust is key. It takes time and effort to foster the trust that provides the foundation for a productive and meaningful relationship. You don't have to be best friends with everyone you meet, but it's crucial to show that you care and that you are invested in adding value to your relationships.

Different Types of Relationships

Relationships can come in different forms. Each connection leads to learning, growth, and professional development. Here are some of the fundamental types of relationships you can build:

❖   Professional relationships: These are the relationships you form with people in your industry or field. They may include colleagues, business partners, or vendors. Cultivating professional relationships allows you to stay updated on industry trends and learn from those who have similar interests and goals.

❖ Mentor relationships: Mentors are trusted advisors who have expert knowledge or significant experience in a particular field. They can help guide your career growth and provide guidance in areas where you have less experience.

❖ Personal relationships: Networking doesn't need to be all about business. You can build meaningful connections through shared interests and hobbies. These relationships can provide emotional and mental support and give you a chance to relax and recharge.

Listening and Showing Empathy

One crucial aspect of building productive relationships is actively listening and understanding the needs of the other person. People appreciate when others take the time to listen to what they have to say. Pay attention to the other person's responses, and try to read between the lines, which indicates the person's innermost thoughts.

Just as valuable is showing empathy - understanding and genuinely caring about the concerns and challenges of others. Empathy helps to create a deeper bond and encourages trust, building the foundation for positive relationships.

Demonstrating Trustworthiness

Trust is key in any relationship, and it is an essential value that should be demonstrated in the business world. It's better to ensure the trust by acting in a manner that inspires this sentiment from the other person. Make sure always to follow through on promises and commitments and be transparent and honest in your dealings. By showing that you can be trusted, you strengthen the foundation of the relationship.

Finding Ways to Add Value

Another integral part of relationship-building is finding ways to add value. What can you offer that would be beneficial to the other person? It can be as simple as giving a referral or sharing an article or blog post that's relevant to their interests or needs.

Think about what the other person needs and how you can help. When you provide value, you show that you care about the other person and are invested in their success. By helping others to achieve their goals, you build relationships that can withstand the challenges and obstacles of the business world.

Maintaining Regular Communication

Regular communication is a vital key to building strong and enduring relationships. Consistency is crucial in maintaining the relationship's health, meaning that you should keep checking up on the people in your network and providing continued support as needed. It can be as simple as a quick email or message, or a scheduled catch-up call or meeting.

The same rule applies once in a while, catch-ups provide a platform to check how your network is doing, offer assistance and get to know them better.

Addressing Conflicts or Challenges

In all relationships, there will come a time when conflicts or challenges arise. It's how you handle those situations that determine the strength and depth of your relationship. Be open, honest, and direct when addressing problems, and try to find a mutually beneficial solution.

Approaching conflicts with an open and transparent mind can improve the situation and build a stronger relationship in the long run.

Recognizing and Celebrating Milestones

When someone in your network achieves a milestone, celebrate with them. Let them know that you're proud of them and recognize their hard work and dedication. Celebrating together provides an opportunity to strengthen your relationships by acknowledging the shared experiences.

Take time to celebrate others' achievements as if it was your own, do so in a genuine and sincere way. Giving credit to others shows your goodwill and makes people feel appreciated and valued.

The Bottom-line

Building relationships is a fundamental aspect of networking. Whether it's finding ways to add value, listening and showing empathy, demonstrating trustworthiness, or celebrating milestones, investing time and effort into creating genuine connections is a worthy endeavor. By creating a network of trusted allies who share your vision and values, you will enter a strong position to accomplish your personal and professional goals.

CHAPTER 6: USING SOCIAL MEDIA FOR NETWORKING

In today's world, social media platforms have become an integral part of our lives. Given their widespread use, it's not surprising that social media can be an excellent tool for networking. With millions of active users, platforms like LinkedIn, Twitter, and Facebook serve as valuable resources for meeting new people, building relationships, and expanding your network. In this chapter, we will explore ways to leverage social media for networking and personal branding.

Overview of Popular Social Media Platforms

Among the most popular social media platforms for networking today are LinkedIn, Twitter, and Facebook. Each platform has its unique features, target audience, and benefits:

LinkedIn is a professional networking site that allows you to connect with other professionals, potential employers, and clients. It's an excellent platform for job seekers and those who want to expand their business networks. You can create a personal profile, highlight your skills and experiences, and follow companies or groups relevant to your interests.

Twitter offers a great way to build brand awareness, engage with followers, and generate leads. It's an effective platform for sharing quick insights, links to articles, and engaging in industry-related conversations. With tweets being limited to 280 characters, Twitter encourages concise communication and highlights your ability to communicate effectively.

Facebook provides a more casual environment to connect with friends and family but is also an excellent platform to build communities around shared interests and hobbies. You can join groups related to your industry, attend virtual events, and engage in conversations with others interested in the same topics.

Identifying the Right Platforms for Your Goals

To optimize your social media networking efforts, it's essential to identify the right platforms for your goals. Consider your target audience, the type of content you want to share, and what you hope to achieve. Once you determine this, you can then create a social media strategy that aligns with your networking goals.

Building a Strong Online Presence

To fully leverage social media for networking, it's important to build a strong online presence. Here are some tips on how to do this effectively:

1. Create a professional profile

Whether you're using LinkedIn, Twitter, or Facebook, creating a complete and professional-looking profile is critical. Make sure to use a clear profile picture, fill out your bio/description with your relevant experience, and include a link to your website or other relevant social media profiles.

2. Share valuable content

Sharing valuable content establishes you as a thought leader in your industry. Share articles, whitepapers, infographics, and other content relevant to your target audience.

3. Engage with others

Engaging with other professionals and thought leaders through commenting and sharing their content is a great way to start building relationships. Like, share, and comment on their posts, and tag them in relevant conversations.

4. Participate in online communities

Join relevant online groups or communities related to your industry or interests. Engage in conversations and offer helpful insights or resources to members. Being active in these groups can help you make new connections and establish yourself as a valuable resource.

5. Be consistent

Posting regularly and consistently is essential to stay top-of-mind with your connections. Schedule posts in advance, and use a mix of text, links, images, and videos to keep your content fresh.

Direct Messaging and Email Etiquette

When communicating with others on social media, it's important to follow best practices for direct messaging and email etiquette. Here are a few tips to keep in mind:

1. Personalize your messages

When reaching out to someone for the first time, introduce yourself, and explain why you would like to connect. Make it clear that you are reaching out because you share a common interest or appreciate what they're doing.

2. Be concise

Respect the person's time by being concise in your message. Keep your message short while still delivering the relevant information.

3. Follow up promptly

If someone responds to your message, respond promptly to continue the conversation. Conversely, if you receive a message but don't have time to respond immediately, let the person know when they can expect a response.

4. Respect their time

When sending an email or direct message, respect the person's time by not asking for too much information at once. Be clear and concise in your communication and remember to express gratitude for any help they provide.

Avoiding Common Social Media Mistakes

Social media is an incredibly powerful tool for networking, but it's essential to avoid common mistakes that can undermine your efforts. Here are some common social media mistakes to avoid:

1. Spamming others

Sending too many messages or posts can be overwhelming and may lead to others unfollowing you.

2. Being overly self-promotional

Constantly promoting yourself or your business can be a turn-off for others. Instead, focus on sharing valuable content and engaging in conversations that add value to your network.

3. Failing to customize your message

Sending the same message to everyone can seem impersonal. Rather than using a cookie-cutter message, take the time to personalize each message specifically for the individual.

Final Thoughts

Social networking sites have revolutionized the way people connect and can greatly benefit an individual's personal and professional growth. To effectively leverage these platforms, one must build a strong online presence, consistently engage by sharing valuable content and resources, and keep in mind the best practices for direct messaging, email etiquette, and avoiding common errors. By doing so, one can harness the power of social media to expand their network and build relationships that will last a lifetime.

CHAPTER 7: NETWORKING FOR CAREER ADVANCEMENT

Networking is an essential step for career advancement and professional growth. Building connections, trust, and relationships with key people opens doors to new opportunities, whether it's getting promoted, finding a new job, or pivoting your career path. Networking can also help you navigate office politics, gain visibility within your organization, and develop your personal brand.

Here are some tips and strategies to help you network effectively for career advancement:

Identifying key decision makers

To advance in your career, you need to understand the decision-making hierarchy within your organization. This means identifying key individuals, such as your boss, senior leaders, and influential colleagues, who have a say in your career progression. Take the time to observe and understand how your organization functions and seek out opportunities to engage with these decision makers.

Building relationships with mentors and sponsors

Having a mentor or a sponsor can be valuable in your career advancement. Mentors are typically more experienced individuals who can provide guidance, advice, and perspective on your career goals. Sponsors, on the other hand, are senior leaders who have the power to advocate for you and open doors to new opportunities. Identifying and building relationships with mentors and sponsors can provide you with invaluable support and help you move up the career ladder.

Finding and applying for job opportunities

Networking can help you explore new job opportunities within or outside of your organization. Attend industry conferences, job fairs, and networking events to meet recruiters and hiring managers. Leverage your connections to find out about job openings and be proactive about applying for roles that align with your career goals.

Navigating office politics

Office politics can be complex and challenging to navigate, but it's essential for career advancement. Build relationships with influential colleagues and be mindful of power dynamics within your organization. Learn to anticipate challenges and opportunities and be strategic in your interactions with others.

Developing a personal development plan

Having a clear plan for your career development is crucial for advancing in your profession. Identify your short-term and long-term goals, areas of strength and weakness, and opportunities for growth. Define the steps you need to take to achieve your goals and track your progress over time.

Communicating your value to employers

Networking can help you articulate your value proposition and communicate your accomplishments and skills to employers. Be prepared to showcase your experience, achievements, and unique selling points when networking with potential employers or colleagues.

Pursuing ongoing learning and professional development

Networking is not just about making connections; it's also about continuous learning and growth. Attend workshops, seminars, and training sessions to enhance your skills and knowledge. Consider pursuing additional education or certifications to increase your credentials and marketability.

Networking for career advancement takes time, effort, and persistence, but the rewards can be significant. By building strong relationships, gaining visibility, and developing your skills, you can position yourself for new opportunities and achieve your career goals.

CHAPTER 8: NETWORKING FOR ENTREPRENEURSHIP

Starting a business can be a daunting task, and as an entrepreneur, it's crucial to understand the importance of networking. Networking can help entrepreneurs in various ways, from finding the right customers and suppliers to overcoming obstacles and setbacks.

This chapter will explore the unique challenges of entrepreneurship and how networking can help entrepreneurs overcome those challenges. Let's dive in!

The unique challenges of entrepreneurship

Entrepreneurship is not for the faint of heart. Starting a business requires a lot of hard work, dedication, and perseverance. Here are some of the challenges that entrepreneurs typically face:

❖ Lack of support: Starting a business can be a lonely journey, and it's essential to have a supportive community to rely on when things get tough.

❖ Financial constraints: Starting a business requires money, and most entrepreneurs start with limited funds.

❖ Lack of expertise: Entrepreneurs wear many hats and

are responsible for various aspects of their business, from marketing to finance.

❖ Managing risk: Starting a business comes with inherent risks, and entrepreneurs have to be comfortable with uncertainty and ambiguity.

❖ Rejection: It's not uncommon for entrepreneurs to face rejection from potential customers, suppliers, investors, or partners.

Finding and building a supportive community

Building a supportive community is crucial for entrepreneurs, as it can provide emotional support, resources, and industry insights. Here are some ways to build a supportive community:

❖ Attend networking events: Networking events are a great way to meet like-minded individuals and potential customers, suppliers, investors, or partners. Look for events that are focused on entrepreneurship or your industry.

❖ Join entrepreneurship organizations: There are many entrepreneurship organizations that provide support and resources to entrepreneurs. Joining these organizations can provide access to valuable resources and a supportive community.

❖ Attend industry conferences: Attending industry conferences can help entrepreneurs stay up-to-date with industry trends and connect with other entrepreneurs in their industry.

❖ Build a team: Building a team of advisors, mentors, and partners can provide critical support and expertise to entrepreneurs.

Developing a business plan

A business plan is a crucial tool for entrepreneurs as it provides a roadmap for their business. A business plan typically includes the following elements:

- ❖ Executive summary: A brief summary of your business plan that highlights the key points.

- ❖ Company overview: An overview of your company, including its mission, vision, and values.

- ❖ Market analysis: A description of your target market, including its size, competition, and trends.

- ❖ Products or services: A description of your products or services, including their features and benefits.

- ❖ Marketing and sales: A description of how you plan to market and sell your products or services.

- ❖ Financial projections: A projection of your financial performance, including sales, expenses, and profits.

Building relationships with customers and suppliers

Building relationships with customers and suppliers is critical for entrepreneurs as it can provide a competitive advantage and help them grow their business. Here are some tips for building relationships with customers and suppliers:

- ❖ Communicate regularly: Communicate regularly with your customers and suppliers to build trust and stay top-of-mind.

- ❖ Deliver on your promises: Deliver on your promises to build a reputation for reliability and excellence.

- ❖ Ask for feedback: Ask your customers and suppliers for feedback to improve your products or services.

- ❖ Be flexible: Be flexible with your customers and suppliers to build long-term relationships.

Overcoming obstacles and setbacks

Entrepreneurship comes with its fair share of obstacles and setbacks. Here are some ways to overcome them:

❖ Build resilience: Building resilience is crucial for entrepreneurs as it can help them overcome setbacks and stay focused on their goals.

❖ Seek inspiration: Seeking inspiration from other successful entrepreneurs can provide motivation and insight.

❖ Be resourceful: Being resourceful and finding creative solutions to problems can help entrepreneurs overcome obstacles.

❖ Learn from failures: Learning from failures can provide valuable lessons and help entrepreneurs improve their business.

Scaling your business through networking

Scaling a business requires a lot of effort, and networking can play a significant role in helping entrepreneurs expand their business. Here are some ways to scale your business through networking:

❖ Find new customers: Networking events can provide access to potential customers and help entrepreneurs expand their customer base.

❖ Build partnerships: Building partnerships can provide access to new markets, products, and resources.

❖ Meet investors: Networking events can provide access to potential investors and help entrepreneurs secure funding for their business.

❖ attract talent: Entrepreneurs can meet potential employees at networking events and build relationships with them.

Navigating legal and financial considerations

Entrepreneurs have to navigate various legal and financial considerations as they start and grow their business. Here are some tips for navigating these considerations:

❖   Consult with a lawyer: Consulting with a lawyer can provide guidance on legal issues, such as business registration, contracts, and intellectual property.

❖   Hire a financial advisor: Hiring a financial advisor can provide guidance on financial issues, such as taxation and accounting.

❖   Build a strong team: Building a team of experts, such as a lawyer, accountant, and financial advisor, can provide critical support and expertise.

Establishing a personal brand as an entrepreneur

Establishing a personal brand is crucial for entrepreneurs as it can help them stand out in a crowded market and attract customers, investors, and partners. Here are some tips for establishing a personal brand:

❖   Develop a consistent visual identity: Developing a consistent visual identity, such as a logo and website, can help entrepreneurs establish a strong brand identity.

❖   Share your values: Sharing your values can help entrepreneurs build trust and credibility with their customers and partners.

❖   Produce valuable content: Producing valuable content, such as blogs, videos, or podcasts, can help entrepreneurs establish themselves as thought leaders in their industry.

❖   Engage with your audience: Engaging with your audience, such as through social media or events, can help entrepreneurs build a loyal following.

Conclusion

Networking can provide crucial support and resources for entrepreneurs as they start and grow their business. From building a supportive community to overcoming obstacles and setbacks, networking can play a significant role in the success of entrepreneurs. By following the tips and strategies outlined in this chapter, entrepreneurs can establish a strong personal brand and scale their business through networking.

CHAPTER 9: NETWORKING FOR SALES AND BUSINESS DEVELOPMENT

Sales and business development are essential components of any successful business. Networking is one of the most efficient and effective ways to identify new customers, build relationships with them, and ultimately close deals. The process can be daunting, especially for those who are new to the sales process or who may not be comfortable with networking. In this chapter, we'll explore how networking can be used successfully in sales and business development.

Understanding the Sales Process

To start, it's important to understand the sales process. Sales is simply the process of identifying potential customers, building relationships with them, understanding their needs and challenges, and offering solutions that meet those needs. The sales process typically involves several stages, from prospecting (identifying potential customers), to lead qualification (assessing potential customers' interest and ability to purchase), and ultimately to closing the deal.

Networking is an essential part of the sales process because it provides opportunities to identify potential customers and build the relationships that are necessary for closing deals. Successful networking involves building rapport with potential customers, establishing credibility, and ultimately gaining their trust.

Building Rapport with Potential Clients

Building rapport with potential clients involves demonstrating genuine interest in their business and their needs. This can be accomplished by asking open-ended questions that encourage conversation and show a willingness to listen. It's also important to find common ground, such as shared interests or experiences, in order to establish a connection.

In addition to asking questions, it's important to be a good listener. Active listening involves paying close attention to what the potential client is saying and responding in a way that demonstrates understanding. This can help build empathy and trust, which are essential components of any successful business relationship.

Conducting Effective Sales Meetings

Networking often leads to sales meetings, where potential clients have the opportunity to learn more about your business and the solutions you offer. To conduct effective sales meetings, it's important to be well-prepared. This involves doing research on the potential client, understanding their needs and challenges, and identifying how your solutions can help.

During the meeting itself, it's important to stay focused on the potential client's needs and challenges. This means asking targeted questions, actively listening to their responses, and providing solutions that are tailored to their specific situation.

Identifying Customer Pain Points

In order to provide effective solutions to potential clients, it's essential to identify their pain points. Pain points are the challenges or problems that potential customers are experiencing in their business that your solutions can help alleviate. Identifying pain points involves asking questions about their business, understanding their goals, and assessing their current situation.

Developing Compelling Proposals

Once you've identified potential clients' pain points, it's time to develop compelling proposals that address their specific needs and challenges. A good proposal should be clear, concise, and tailored to the potential client's situation. It should also include a clear value proposition that outlines the benefits that your solutions provide.

Handling Objections and Negotiation

Inevitably, potential clients may have objections or concerns regarding your solutions. It's important to be prepared for these objections and to respond in a way that addresses their concerns while also demonstrating the value of your solutions. Good negotiation skills are also important in the sales process, as they allow you to find common ground and reach mutually beneficial agreements.

Closing Deals Successfully

Ultimately, the goal of networking in sales and business development is to close deals successfully. This involves demonstrating the value of your solutions, establishing trust and credibility with potential clients, and negotiating effectively. Successful networking and sales require a long-term approach that involves building relationships and maintaining them over time.

Building Long-Term Customer Relationships

Networking is not just about identifying new customers, it's also about building long-term relationships with them. Repeat business and referrals are essential components of any successful business. This means that it's important to maintain regular communication with customers, address any concerns or challenges they may have, and find ways to add value to their business.

Conclusion

Networking is an essential component of sales and business development. It provides opportunities to identify potential customers, build relationships with them, and ultimately close deals successfully. Successful networking requires building rapport with potential clients, conducting effective sales meetings, identifying customer pain points, developing compelling proposals, handling objections and negotiation, and building long-term customer relationships. By mastering these skills, anyone can use networking to achieve success in sales and business development.

CHAPTER 10: NETWORKING FOR SOCIAL IMPACT

Networking can have a significant impact on individuals and organizations beyond their personal and professional growth. It can lead to positive change in society, environment, and various social issues. In this chapter, we will discuss the role of networking in social impact and how to utilize networking skills for positive change.

Identifying opportunities to make a difference

One of the main benefits of networking for social impact is the ability to connect with like-minded individuals and organizations. By attending networking events, joining groups and associations, and utilizing social media platforms, you can identify opportunities to get involved and make a difference. You may discover organizations that align with your values and goals, or individuals who are passionate about similar causes. It's important to approach networking with an open mind and be willing to listen and learn about different perspectives and approaches to social impact.

Building relationships with like-minded individuals and organizations

Once you have identified opportunities to make a difference, the next step is to build relationships with individuals and organizations that share your passion for social impact. Networking events, online communities, and volunteer opportunities are great ways to connect with like-minded people. It's important to approach networking with authenticity and genuine interest in learning about others and their work. Building strong relationships based on trust and shared goals is key to creating lasting change.

Raising awareness and funds for social causes

Networking can be a powerful tool for raising awareness and funds for social causes. By leveraging your connections, you can spread the word about important issues and initiatives and encourage others to get involved. Social media platforms offer numerous opportunities to share information and raise awareness, through posts, videos, and campaigns. You can also utilize your personal and professional network to fundraise for social causes, by organizing events or leveraging crowdfunding platforms.

Leveraging social media for campaigns

Social media can be a powerful tool for organizing and promoting social campaigns. By utilizing various platforms, you can reach a wider audience and engage with individuals who share your values. Social media campaigns can take various forms, such as hashtags, challenges, and online petitions. The key to successful social media campaigns is to create engaging content that resonates with your audience and encourages them to take action.

Advocating for policy change

Networking can also be utilized to advocate for policy change related to social issues. By connecting with individuals and organizations that share your goals, you can mobilize a collective voice and advocate for systemic change. This can take various forms, such as attending advocacy events, contacting elected officials, and organizing collaborative campaigns. Building strategic alliances and coalitions is key to creating meaningful impact through policy change.

Measuring impact and creating sustainability

Networking for social impact requires a long-term approach, focused on measuring impact and creating sustainability. It's important to track progress and evaluate the effectiveness of networking initiatives and make adjustments as needed. Sustainability requires building resilient networks, focused on creating meaningful change over time. This can involve adopting innovative solutions, leveraging technology, and collaborating across sectors and industries.

Collaborating for greater impact

Finally, collaboration is key to maximizing the impact of networking for social impact. By building relationships and partnerships with individuals and organizations across different sectors and industries, you can leverage collective knowledge, skills, and resources. Collaboration requires being open to different perspectives and approaches and being willing to adopt new solutions and methods. By working together, we can create meaningful change and contribute to a brighter future for all.

In conclusion, networking can have a powerful impact on social issues and contribute to positive change in our world. By identifying opportunities, building strong relationships, leveraging social media, advocating for policy change, measuring impact, and collaborating across sectors and industries, we can create sustainable solutions and build a brighter future for all.

CHAPTER 11: BUILDING A POWERFUL NETWORK

Networking is about building relationships with others for mutual professional and personal benefits. A network can help you achieve your goals, support you in your endeavors, and provide valuable connections. Building a powerful network requires focus, strategy, and effort. In this chapter, we will discuss the key elements of building a powerful network and how to leverage it for mutual benefit.

Creating a diverse and inclusive network

A powerful network is one that is diverse and inclusive. Diversity refers to the range of differences among people, including but not limited to race, ethnicity, gender, age, religion, sexual orientation, and national origin. Inclusion is the act of creating an environment where all individuals are valued and respected. By creating a network that reflects diversity and inclusivity, you are expanding your horizons, learning from different perspectives, and appreciating different experiences and backgrounds.

Identifying potential allies and champions

An ally is someone who actively supports and advocates for another person or group. Champions, on the other hand, are individuals who go above and beyond in supporting and promoting others. Both allies and champions can significantly influence your career and help your network grow. To identify potential allies and champions, you need to consider those who share your values, vision, and ambitions. These individuals may include colleagues, mentors, sponsors, friends, or family members. Reach out to them and express your appreciation for their support. Also, be willing to reciprocate and support them whenever possible.

Building a network of mentors and advisors

Mentors and advisors are invaluable resources that can provide guidance, wisdom, and perspective. A mentor is someone with experience and expertise in your field who can offer advice, support, and guidance to help you achieve your goals. An advisor, on the other hand, is someone who provides specific expertise or counsel. To build a network of mentors and advisors, you need to be proactive in seeking out individuals who have the expertise and knowledge you seek. Attend professional events, join mentorship programs, or seek out individuals who you admire and respect.

Diversifying your network across industries and sectors

A powerful network is one that offers diversity in terms of industry, sector, and geography. By expanding your network to include individuals from different industries, you expose yourself to new ideas, trends, and opportunities. Additionally, networking across sectors can help you to identify and leverage transferable skills and experiences. Seek out events and organizations outside of your industry or sector to meet new people and learn about new perspectives.

Developing a strategic referral system

Referrals are a powerful way to grow your network. A referral is an introduction to someone who can help you achieve your goals, or whom you can help in turn. Referrals can be made by colleagues, friends, family members, mentors, or clients. To develop a strategic referral system, you need to identify and cultivate relationships with individuals who can make valuable introductions. Reach out to them regularly to provide updates on your progress, express gratitude, and ask for advice.

Nurturing relationships with influencers

An influencer is someone who has the power to influence others' opinions or decisions. Influencers can be industry leaders, thought leaders, or social media personalities. To nurture relationships with influencers, you need to be active in your industry or sector, share valuable content, and contribute to conversations where influencers participate. Reach out to them to offer insights or ask for advice but respect their time and boundaries.

Leveraging your network for mutual benefit

A powerful network is one that benefits all of its members. By leveraging your network for mutual benefit, you create a culture of generosity and reciprocity. When you help someone else achieve their goals, they are more likely to help you in turn. To leverage your network effectively, you need to identify areas where you can add value to others, such as introducing them to potential clients or providing recommendations. Additionally, be willing to ask for help when you need it.

Creating a culture of generosity and reciprocity

Finally, creating a culture of generosity and reciprocity is the key to building a powerful network. When you approach networking with an attitude of giving and sharing, you create an environment where others are more likely to do the same. By nurturing relationships with others and providing value, you build trust and respect, which are essential for cultivating a powerful network.

Conclusion

Building a powerful network takes time, effort, and strategy. By creating a diverse and inclusive network, identifying potential allies and champions, building a network of mentors and advisors, diversifying your network, developing a strategic referral system, nurturing relationships with influencers, leveraging your network for mutual benefit, and creating a culture of generosity and reciprocity, you can maximize the power of your network. Mastering these skills requires ongoing effort and a commitment to lifelong learning and growth. By embracing the power of personal and professional relationships, you can achieve your goals and make a meaningful difference in the world.

CHAPTER 12: NETWORKING DOS AND DON'TS

Networking is an essential aspect of personal and professional growth. It provides an excellent opportunity to connect with people who can offer valuable insights, support, and opportunities. However, networking can be tricky, and one wrong move can ruin everything. Therefore, it is crucial to learn the dos and don'ts when it comes to networking. In this chapter, I will share some common mistakes to avoid in networking and highlight some best practices.

Common mistakes to avoid in networking

❖ Being too self-centered: It's okay to talk about your achievements and goals, but it is also important to show interest in other people's lives and work.

❖ Not being prepared: If you're attending an event or a meeting, make sure you have enough business cards, your elevator pitch is ready, and you've done your research about the people you're going to meet.

❖ Ignoring body language: Your body language says a lot about you and your intentions. Be mindful of how you present yourself and the signals you're sending.

❖ Not following up: Meeting people and exchanging business

cards is just the first step. The real work begins after the event when you need to follow up with the people you've met.

❖   Over-promoting yourself: It's essential to show your value proposition, but it should be done in a subtle and respectful way.

❖   Being pushy: Don't try to force any agendas or sales down someone's throat. Instead, build a natural relationship.

❖   Forgetting to be authentic: Authenticity is crucial to establishing long-term relationships. People can sense when someone is being fake or insincere.

Best practices for networking

❖   Be respectful of others' time and boundaries: People are busy, and they have their own schedules. Make sure to respect their time and never overstay your welcome.

❖   Follow up promptly and professionally: If you've promised to follow up with someone, do so promptly, and in the way that you've agreed upon. It's a good idea to keep things concise and professional.

❖   Show gratitude and appreciation: When someone has done something nice for you, don't forget to express your appreciation. A simple thank you can go a long way.

❖   Be authentic and transparent: People value honesty and authenticity, so be genuine in your interactions.

❖   Be respectful of different backgrounds and cultures: Diversity and inclusion are crucial in any field. Be mindful of the cultural differences when networking and make an effort to be inclusive.

❖   Listen actively: Networking is an excellent opportunity to learn from others, so listen carefully to what people have to say. Active listening means focusing on the speaker instead of thinking about what you're going to say next.

❖ Show empathy: Networking is all about building relationships, and empathy is key to understanding and connecting with other people.

❖ Be mindful of body language and presentation: Your body language can say as much as your words. Be mindful of how you present yourself and the signals you're sending.

❖ Be authentic, but professional: Networking is all about connecting with people in a professional setting, so make sure to maintain a level of professionalism in your conversations.

❖ Always be learning and growing Networking is an ongoing process, and there is always something new to learn. Be open to new ideas and be willing to learn from others.

Conclusion

Networking is not just about connecting with people and exchanging business cards. It's about building genuine relationships that can lead to long-term personal and professional growth. By following the dos and don'ts of networking, you can establish meaningful connections with people in your field and beyond. It's essential to be respectful, authentic, and professional in all your interactions. Just remember to take your time, be patient, and be open to new opportunities and challenges.

CHAPTER 13: NETWORKING USING VIRTUAL TOOLS

With the increasing trend of remote work and online communication, virtual networking has become a crucial part of building and maintaining relationships in the digital age. In this chapter, we'll explore the different virtual networking tools available and how to use them effectively.

Overview of Virtual Networking Tools

Virtual networking tools come in various forms, from social media platforms and professional networking sites to video conferencing software and online communities. Each tool has its unique features and benefits, so it's essential to choose the right platform for your networking goals.

LinkedIn, for example, is the most popular professional networking site used by businesses and professionals worldwide. You can use it to showcase your skills and experience, connect with industry peers, and access job opportunities. Twitter and Facebook are also useful social media platforms for networking, especially for building personal connections with potential clients or collaborators.

Video conferencing tools like Zoom and Skype are excellent for face-to-face virtual networking, enabling you to have virtual meetings and attend virtual events from anywhere, anytime. Online communities like LinkedIn groups or Slack channels are also great resources for connecting with like-minded individuals and engaging in discussions on relevant topics.

Choosing the Right Platform for Your Goals

To use virtual networking tools effectively, you need to choose the right platform that aligns with your networking goals. If you're looking to expand your professional network and gain industry insights, LinkedIn is an excellent platform to start. You can join relevant LinkedIn groups, participate in industry discussions, and connect with professionals in your field.

If you're an entrepreneur looking to build a following and connect with customers, Twitter and Facebook are great platforms to engage in conversations, share valuable insights, and promote your business.

For virtual meetings or events, video conferencing software like Zoom and Skype offer a comprehensive range of features and tools that enable you to have face-to-face interactions with people from all over the world.

One essential consideration when choosing virtual networking tools is security and privacy. It's vital to use platforms that guarantee the privacy of your data and protect you from cyber threats.

Building a Strong Online Presence

Building a strong online presence is crucial to virtual networking success. Your online presence should communicate your brand and showcase your skills and experience. To build a strong online presence, you need to:

❖   Create a complete profile: Fill in all the essential details of your profile, including your education, work experience, and skills.

❖   Use keywords: Use relevant keywords for your field to optimize your profile.

❖   Share valuable content: Share valuable insights, articles, and resources that align with your networking goals.

❖   Engage with others: Engage with other professionals in your field by commenting on their posts or sharing their content.

❖   Stay active: Regularly update your profile, share new content, and interact with other users to keep your profile active and visible.

Engaging with Others Virtually

Engaging with others virtually can be challenging, but it's essential to building valuable connections and nurturing relationships. When engaging with others virtually, consider the following tips:

❖   Be polite and professional: Always be polite and professional in your communication, even if it's informal.

❖   Listen actively: Listen to what others have to say and respond thoughtfully.

❖   Show empathy: Show empathy by acknowledging others' feelings and opinions.

❖   Ask open-ended questions: Ask open-ended questions that encourage conversation and reflection.

❖   Use appropriate body language: Use appropriate body language when on video conferencing software and convey confidence and professionalism.

❖   Avoid distractions: Ensure that you're in a quiet and

distraction-free environment when engaging with others virtually.

Hosting and Attending Virtual Events

Virtual events, such as webinars, conferences, and seminars, provide an excellent opportunity to connect with people and access industry knowledge from the comfort of your home. When hosting or attending virtual events, consider the following tips:

❖ Be prepared: Prepare relevant questions or contributions to make to the event.

❖ Dress professionally: Follow professional dress codes for video conferencing software.

❖ Use appropriate behavior: Be courteous and professional during the event.

❖ Take notes: Take notes and summarize the key takeaways from the event.

❖ Follow up: Follow up with the speakers or attendees after the event to thank them for their time and build a connection.

Overcoming the Challenges of Virtual Networking

While virtual networking offers many benefits, it also comes with its unique challenges. Some common challenges include:

❖ Technical difficulties: Technical difficulties such as bad internet connection can affect the quality of virtual networking.

❖ Limited social cues: Virtual networking limits social cues, making it harder to communicate effectively.

❖ Reduced attention span: Virtual networking can be more challenging to maintain focus than in-person networking, which requires more active attention.

To overcome these challenges, it's essential to be patient, flexible and focus on building authentic connections.

Maintaining Security and Privacy

As virtual networking becomes more prevalent, it's crucial to maintain security and privacy when using virtual networking tools. Here are some tips to help you stay safe:

❖ Use secure platforms: Use platforms that offer end-to-end encryption and guarantee the privacy of your data.

❖ Use strong passwords: Use strong passwords and enable two-factor authentication to enhance your account security.

❖ Avoid clicking suspicious links: Avoid clicking on links from unknown sources and be cautious of phishing attempts.

❖ Review app permissions: Review app permissions before downloading and using virtual networking tools.

❖ Regularly update your software: Regularly update your software to enhance security and fix any security vulnerabilities.

Final Thoughts

Virtual networking is a powerful tool that enables you to build and maintain meaningful relationships online. By choosing the right platform, building a strong online presence, and engaging with others thoughtfully, you can leverage virtual networking for personal and professional growth. Remember to remain patient, flexible, and focused on building authentic connections while staying safe and secure online.

CHAPTER 14: NETWORKING FOR INTERNATIONAL OPPORTUNITIES

In today's globalized world, networking with individuals and organizations abroad has become a critical component of personal and professional growth. Whether you are looking to expand your business overseas, study abroad, or simply build relationships with people from different cultures, networking for international opportunities can be a transformative experience. However, the cultural differences and language barriers can make it challenging to build relationships with individuals from different countries. In this chapter, we will explore some tips and strategies for networking for international opportunities.

Understanding Cultural Norms and Expectations

To successfully network with individuals from different cultures, it is essential to understand their cultural norms and expectations. Culture affects everything from how people communicate and build relationships to their attitudes towards time, hierarchy, and formality. Before you engage with individuals from different cultures, it is important to research their cultural norms and etiquette. For example, in some cultures, it is considered impolite to interrupt while others are speaking, while in others, it is acceptable. Similarly, in some cultures, punctuality is highly valued, while in others, a more relaxed attitude towards time may be the norm.

Preparing for Cross-Cultural Communication

In addition to understanding cultural norms, it is important to prepare for cross-cultural communication. This includes developing cross-cultural communication skills such as active listening and interpreting non-verbal cues. It is also helpful to learn some basic phrases in the language of the country you are trying to network in. Even if you are not fluent in the language, making an effort to speak in the local language shows respect and a willingness to learn.

Identifying Opportunities for International Networking

Networking opportunities for international opportunities can be found in a variety of settings. For example, attending international trade shows, conferences, and cultural events are excellent ways to meet individuals from different countries. Additionally, online networking platforms such as LinkedIn and Twitter can help you connect with people from all over the world.

Building Relationships with Individuals and Organizations Abroad

Building relationships with individuals and organizations abroad is similar to building relationships in your own country. Active listening, mutual respect, and shared interests are essential components of building successful relationships. However, because of the cultural differences, it is important to be patient and open-minded when building relationships with people from different cultures. Be respectful of their customs and traditions, and do not make assumptions based on your own cultural background.

Navigating Language Barriers

Language barriers can be a significant challenge when networking for international opportunities. While learning the language of the country you are trying to network in can be helpful, it is not always possible. In some cases, hiring a translator or working with an interpreter can help bridge the communication gap. Additionally, relying on visual aids and non-verbal cues can be helpful when communicating with individuals who speak a different language.

Creating a Targeted Outreach Plan

To make the most of your international networking efforts, it can be helpful to create a targeted outreach plan. This plan should identify your goals for networking in a specific country or region, and the individuals and organizations you would like to connect with. Consider reaching out to them through email, social media, or through personal introductions. Be sure to personalize your outreach efforts and highlight your shared interests and goals.

Developing a Global Mindset

A global mindset is essential for successful networking for international opportunities. This means being open-minded, curious, and interested in learning about different cultures and perspectives. Engage in meaningful discussions with people from different countries and ask questions to gain insights into their experiences and beliefs. Be respectful of their customs, and always strive to learn more about the world around you.

Leveraging Technology for Global Networking

Advancements in technology have made global networking more accessible than ever before. From video conferencing to virtual events, there are many ways to connect with individuals from different countries. Utilize online platforms and tools to build relationships, share ideas, and gain insights into different cultures and perspectives. However, be mindful of the different time zones, and respect cultural expectations around communication.

In conclusion, networking for international opportunities can be a rewarding and transformative experience. While the cultural differences and language barriers can make it challenging, it is essential to understand and respect these differences to build successful relationships. By developing cross-cultural communication skills, identifying opportunities for international networking, and creating a targeted outreach plan, you can expand your network and gain insights into different cultures and perspectives. Additionally, cultivating a global mindset and leveraging technology for global networking can help you build relationships with individuals and organizations abroad.

CHAPTER 15: BUILDING A SUPPORTIVE NETWORK

Networking is not just about building transactional relationships with professionals, acquaintances or employers that can help you push your career forward. It's also about building a supportive network that can help you through difficult times and support your personal growth and development. The supportive network can come in the form of a group of peers, friends, mentors, or mastermind groups.

The Role of Support in Networking

One of the most important roles of support in networking is to provide a safe and uplifting environment that can help you build your confidence, learn from others' experiences and develop your skills. It's easy to feel isolated and discouraged in the world of networking, where competition and comparison can feel overwhelming. In such a situation, a supportive network can be the antidote. Here are some tips on how to build a supportive network:

Identifying Sources of Emotional and Mental Support

Life can be tough, and there are times when you need people who can provide emotional and mental support. These individuals could be family, friends, or colleagues who are willing to listen, provide encouragement, or offer a word of advice. It's essential to identify these individuals and build a relationship with them. Open up, communicate, and be vulnerable with them to develop a strong relationship.

Building Relationships with Peers and Colleagues

Networking with peers and colleagues can provide professional support and motivation towards achieving common career goals. In this case, it's essential to find colleagues that share the same interests, values, and aspirations as you. Building a supportive relationship with peers could involve sharing knowledge, collaborating on projects or joining a mastermind group.

Creating a Mastermind Group

Mastermind groups bring like-minded individuals together to share ideas, leverage each other's experiences, and grow together. Members of mastermind groups can provide professional, personal, and emotional support to each other in the pursuit of common goals. A mastermind group is a safe space where individuals can open up about their fears, challenges, aspirations, and celebrate each other's achievements.

Engaging in Mentorship and Coaching

Mentorship and coaching offer a structured relationships that can provide professional and personal support and guidance. Mentors and coaches are individuals who have already achieved what you're looking to achieve and can offer insights and advice on the best strategies to pursue your goals. A mentor or coach can help you identify your weaknesses, build on your strengths, hold you accountable for achieving your goals, and offer constructive feedback when required.

Navigating Difficult or Toxic Relationships

Sometimes we encounter relationships that are challenging or even toxic. For example, we could meet individuals that are overly competitive, dismissive, or hostile. Such relationships have the potential to damage our morale and lead to negative effects on our personal and professional lives. One way to navigate such relationships is by setting boundaries, finding ways to limit interactions, or finding alternative relationships. In some cases, it might be worth addressing the issue directly to see if there's a possibility to reconcile the relationship.

Cultivating a Positive and Uplifting Network

Networking can be challenging, and sometimes we encounter individuals who are negative and demotivating. In such cases, it's essential to cultivate a positive and uplifting network that can counteract the negative energy. Such a network should include individuals that appreciate your talents, are supportive of your goals, and are willing to cheer you on. Whenever possible, try to avoid individuals who consistently undermine your confidence or lack enthusiasm for your goals.

Conclusion

Building a supportive network is an essential part of networking. It provides emotional, personal, and professional support that can help you navigate tough times, build your confidence, and achieve your goals. Identifying sources of emotional and personal support, building relationships with peers and colleagues, creating a mastermind group, engaging in mentorship and coaching, navigating difficult or toxic relationships, and cultivating a positive and uplifting network are all critical steps towards building a supportive network. Remember, building a supportive network takes time and effort, but the rewards are immeasurable.

CHAPTER 16: NETWORKING FOR PERSONAL GROWTH

Networking is not just about building professional connections or chasing career goals. It's also an excellent means of personal growth. Meeting new people, learning new things, and exchanging ideas can be instrumental in discovering new perspectives, developing new skills, and overcoming personal barriers.

In this chapter, we will explore how networking can benefit you personally and how to approach the process with a growth mindset.

Finding Like-Minded Individuals for Shared Interests

Networking isn't always about creating professional connections; it can also help you connect with people who share similar interests or hobbies. Perhaps you're interested in gardening, cooking, skydiving, or yoga. Whatever it is, finding like-minded individuals who share similar passions can broaden your world and introduce you to new experiences.

Networking can help you find an interest group or community that matches your preferences and allows you to engage in personal growth actively. Websites like Meetup or Eventbrite allow users to search for groups that match their interests and also host events that foster connections among attendees.

Building Supportive Relationships in Personal Life

Just like you can develop professional relationships through networking, it's possible to create personal relationships too. Personal connections are integral for mental well-being, and establishing a supportive network can be beneficial when navigating everyday life's ups and downs.

Networking outside of your professional circle, such as joining clubs, taking classes, or attending meetups, is an excellent way to meet people in different walks of life. These new relationships can evolve into a supportive network that you can rely on during times of adversity.

Learning about New Cultures and Perspectives

Networking can also provide a unique opportunity to learn about different cultures and ways of life. When you participate in networking opportunities with people from different backgrounds, you get a glimpse into the way they live, work and interact.

Embracing this diversity can widen your viewpoint, enhance your empathy, and broaden your understanding of different cultures. You can learn a lot from others who have diverse perspectives and can expand your world vision, making you a more well-rounded person.

Developing New Skills and Hobbies

There are endless opportunities to learn new skills or pick up new hobbies through networking. Apart from the chance to create personal connections, networking can also be a chance to learn new things. You can expand your knowledge base by attending workshops, online seminars, or conferences related to your interests.

Also, networking can help you build new skills by finding people who exhibit traits that you may need to work on personally or professionally. You can ask questions, attend mentor-ship programs, and learn from those more experienced than you, providing a solid foundation for personal growth.

Overcoming Personal Obstacles with Support

Building a supportive network can also be instrumental in overcoming personal obstacles. Life can pose challenges that you might not necessarily be equipped to handle alone, but through networking, you can find individuals who might have been in similar situations, offering a new perspective or a listening ear.

Whether you are dealing with a personal tragedy, navigating difficult relationships, or struggling with addiction, connecting with individuals who have gone through similar situations can be empowering. Networking offers you the chance to develop an extensive support system that can be a source of hope and strength, guiding you through the tough times.

Embracing Vulnerability and Growth

Choosing vulnerability and opening up to new people is an act of bravery and strength. It can be scary to step out of your comfort zone and embrace change, but networking provides an excellent opportunity to do so.

Embracing vulnerability can lead to significant personal growth as you confront aspects of yourself that you might not have been aware of before. By being open to new people and experiences, you allow yourself to be exposed to fresh perspectives and ideas that have the potential to change your life for the better.

Conclusion

Networking provides a unique and valuable opportunity for personal growth. It allows you to connect with people who share your interests, learn about new cultures and perspectives, develop new skills, and find support when navigating life's challenges. By being open to new experiences and embracing vulnerability, you can expand your world and discover exciting new opportunities for personal growth and development.

CHAPTER 17: NETWORKING FOR CAREER TRANSITIONS

Career transitions can be difficult and intimidating, especially if you're unsure of how to go about it. Networking can help make the transition smoother and faster. This chapter is aimed at individuals who are looking to make a career change or transition and are seeking guidance on how to navigate this process.

Assessing Your Current Career and Identifying Goals

Before you start networking for a career transition, you need to assess your current career, identify your strengths and weaknesses, and decide what you want to achieve in your new career. You should identify the skills and experiences you have that are transferable to your new career. Once you have an understanding of your skillset and what you want to achieve, you can identify target industries and companies.

Building a Roadmap for Your Transition

Once you've defined your goals and target industries, you need to build a roadmap for your transition. A roadmap for a career transition involves defining milestones, breaking down the transition process into smaller steps, and setting deadlines for achieving your milestones. This roadmap will help you stay focused and on track throughout the transition process.

Identifying Transferable Skills and Experiences

Transferable skills are skills that can be transferred and applied across different industries and careers. For example, if you have experience leading a team in your current position, that experience can be applied to a variety of different roles. Identifying your transferable skills and experiences will help you build a compelling case for yourself when networking for career transitions.

Networking with Individuals in Your Target Industry

Once you've defined your goals, identified target industries, and mapped out your transition, the next step is to start networking with individuals in your target industry. Attend industry events, conferences, and meetups to connect with people who are already working in the field you want to transition to. You can also leverage social media platforms like LinkedIn to connect with individuals in your target industry.

Gaining Experience through Internships and Volunteering

Internships and volunteering can provide valuable experience and exposure to your target industry. By participating in internships or volunteering, you can learn new skills, gain hands-on experience, and build a network of contacts in your target industry. These experiences can help you stand out from other candidates when applying for job opportunities in your new career.

Finding and Applying for Job Opportunities

Networking can help you find job opportunities in your target industry. By building relationships with individuals in your target industry, you can learn about job openings and get referrals that may give you an advantage in the application process. You can also leverage job search engines and recruitment websites to identify job opportunities that fit your skills and goals.

Creating a Personal Brand for Your New Career

As you make your transition, it's important to create a personal brand that aligns with your new career goals. This involves developing a clear understanding of your unique value proposition and creating a consistent visual identity across your personal brand. It's important to showcase your transferable skills and experiences in your personal brand, so that potential employers can see the value you bring to the table.

Navigating Challenges During a Career Transition

Networking can help make a career transition smoother, but challenges may still arise. It's important to be patient, resilient, and stay motivated throughout the process. You may face challenges like rejection, lack of experience, or difficulty in identifying job opportunities. Networking can help you navigate these challenges by providing emotional support, mentorship, and access to resources and job opportunities.

Conclusion

Career transitions can be daunting, but networking can help make the process smoother and faster. By assessing your current career, identifying goals, building a roadmap, identifying transferable skills, networking with individuals in your target industry, gaining experience, finding job opportunities, and creating a personal brand, you can make a successful transition. It's important to stay motivated and resilient throughout the process, and to acknowledge and celebrate your successes along the way. Networking can help you make career transitions that align with your goals and aspirations, and lead to a fulfilling and rewarding career.

CHAPTER 18: NETWORKING FOR DIVERSITY AND INCLUSION

In recent years, diversity and inclusion have become hot topics in all industries, as organizations recognize the importance of creating an environment that welcomes individuals from all walks of life. Networking is an excellent way to promote diversity and inclusion, as it enables individuals to connect and build relationships with people from diverse backgrounds, cultures, and perspectives. In this chapter, we'll explore the role of networking in promoting diversity and inclusion and offer tips on building a diverse and inclusive network.

Understanding privilege and biases

To promote diversity and inclusion through networking, it's crucial to first understand privilege and biases. Privilege refers to the unearned advantages that individuals receive based on their social identity, such as race, gender, sexuality, disability, or socio-economic status. Biases, on the other hand, refer to the unconscious judgments that individuals make about others based on their beliefs, attitudes, and experiences. It's important to understand privilege and biases to ensure that our networking efforts are inclusive and accessible to all individuals.

Creating a diverse and inclusive network

To create a diverse and inclusive network, it's important to be intentional about the individuals with whom you build relationships. Here are some tips to help you build a diverse and inclusive network:

❖ Attend events and groups that align with your values: Seek out events and groups that promote diversity and inclusion. Look for organizations that prioritize diversity, equity, and inclusion and attend events that welcome and celebrate individuals from all backgrounds.

❖ Build relationships with individuals from diverse backgrounds: Be intentional about seeking out individuals from diverse backgrounds and initiating conversations. Listen actively and show empathy and be open to learning about their experiences and perspectives.

❖ Advocate for underrepresented groups: Use your networking skills to promote equity and inclusion in your workplace or industry. Advocate for underrepresented groups and speak out against discrimination and injustice.

❖ Celebrate diversity and differences: Embrace the diversity of your network and celebrate the differences that make us unique. Learn about different cultures, traditions, and perspectives, and support events and initiatives that celebrate diversity.

Promoting equity and inclusion in your workplace

Networking can also be a powerful tool for promoting equity and inclusion in your workplace. Here are some tips to help you promote equity and inclusion in your workplace:

1. Engage in courageous conversations: Be willing to engage in difficult conversations about privilege and bias.

Use your networking skills to initiate conversations that challenge outdated beliefs and attitudes and promote greater understanding.

2. Foster an inclusive workplace culture: Use your network to connect with individuals and organizations that promote diversity and inclusion. Share resources and best practices with your colleagues and work together to create a more inclusive workplace culture.

3. Champion underrepresented groups: Use your networking skills to advocate for underrepresented groups in your workplace. Seek out opportunities to mentor and support individuals from diverse backgrounds and use your influence to promote their professional growth and development.

Measuring and evaluating progress

Finally, it's important to measure and evaluate your progress in promoting diversity and inclusion through networking. Set goals and metrics to assess the diversity of your network and track your progress over time. Use feedback from others to identify areas for improvement and develop a plan to continue building a more diverse and inclusive network.

Conclusion

Networking is a powerful tool for promoting diversity and inclusion in all industries. By being intentional about the individuals with whom we build relationships and advocating for underrepresented groups, we can create a more equitable and inclusive society. Let us use our networking skills to challenge our biases and promote greater understanding, empathy, and support for one another.

CHAPTER 19: NETWORKING FOR MENTAL HEALTH AND WELLBEING

Nearly everyone experiences stress and feelings of burnout at some point in their lives. Networking can be a powerful tool that helps to support and improve our mental and emotional health. In this chapter, we'll explore how networking can help improve mental health, ways to build relationships that support mental health, and how to identify and address mental health issues when they arise.

Importance of Social Support for Mental Health

Individuals who have strong, supportive social networks tend to have better mental health outcomes. They have lower rates of depression, anxiety, and stress, and they are better able to cope with the challenges of life, according to research. Social support comes in many forms, including the emotional, practical, and informational support provided by friends, family, and colleagues.

Networking provides an opportunity to build a strong support system. Through networking, we can create relationships with people who understand the pressures we face and who can provide empathy and support. These relationships can lessen our sense of isolation and provide a sense of belonging.

Building Relationships that Support Mental Health

Networking can be a tool for building relationships that support mental health and wellbeing. Here are some strategies for building supportive relationships:

- ❖ Identify individuals who share your values and interests. When you have a shared interest or passion with someone, it is easier to develop a connection and create a supportive relationship. Identify individuals who share your values and interests and who can provide support.

- ❖ Be vulnerable and authentic. Sharing your struggles with others can help you develop deeper relationships and provide opportunities for empathy and support. Be willing to open up and share your experiences to build stronger relationships.

- ❖ Show empathy and support for others. By demonstrating empathy and support for others, you can create a network of people who are willing and able to provide the same support back to you when needed.

- ❖ Prioritize relationships that support your overall wellbeing. Identify and cultivate relationships that support your overall wellbeing, rather than relationships that contribute to stress or other negative emotions.

Identifying and Addressing Mental Health Issues

Networking can be a powerful tool for identifying and addressing mental health issues. Creating a strong, supportive network can help you identify when you or someone in your network is struggling with mental health issues. Here are some strategies for identifying and addressing mental health issues:

❖   Look for signs of emotional distress. Signs of emotional distress include changes in mood, withdrawing from social situations, increased use of drugs or alcohol, trouble sleeping and changes in appetite. If you notice any of these signs, reach out to that person and offer support.

❖   Encourage seeking professional help. If you or someone you know is struggling with mental health issues, encourage them to seek professional help. This could include seeing a therapist, psychiatrist, or other mental health providers.

❖   Create a safe and supportive environment. When someone is struggling with mental health issues, it can be difficult to reach out for help. Create a safe and supportive environment where people feel comfortable sharing their struggles and seeking help.

❖   Advocate for mental health resources. Advocate for mental health resources in your community or workplace. Encourage the implementation of employee assistance programs, counsellors or therapists, and support groups.

Networking for mental health and wellbeing is an essential aspect of building a supportive network. The relationships we create through networking have a significant impact on our mental health. By prioritizing relationships that support mental health and addressing mental health issues when they arise, we can create strong, supportive networks that improve our overall wellbeing.

CHAPTER 20:
CONCLUSION AND
NEXT STEPS

If you've got this far, you should by now have gained a clear understanding of what networking is, why it is important, and how to network effectively. You have also learned about various types of networking, how to build your personal brand, set networking goals, approach networking events, and build relationships. Moreover, you have gained insights into networking for various purposes such as career advancement, entrepreneurship, sales and business development, social impact, international opportunities, personal growth, career transitions, diversity and inclusion, and mental health and wellbeing.

You have also learned about the dos and don'ts of networking, virtual networking tools, building a supportive network, and networking next steps. Now is the time to reflect on what you have learned and think about your next steps.

Reviewing Key Concepts and Takeaways

To review, networking is about building relationships with people who can help you achieve your goals, both personally and professionally. It is not just about getting what you want from others, but also about giving back, being generous, and showing empathy. Networking can help you with career advancement, entrepreneurship, sales and business development, social impact, personal growth, career transitions, diversity and inclusion, and mental health and wellbeing.

To network effectively, you need to build your personal brand, set networking goals, approach networking events, build relationships, use social media for networking, network for career advancement and entrepreneurship, and maintain a diverse and inclusive network. You should also avoid common mistakes, be mindful of body language and presentation, be respectful of others' time and boundaries, follow up promptly and professionally, show gratitude and appreciation, be authentic and transparent, and avoid unethical and inappropriate behavior.

Celebrating Your Achievements

Celebrating your achievements is an important part of the process. Take a moment to reflect on what you have accomplished in your networking journey so far. Maybe you attended a networking event that made you feel nervous, but you gathered the courage to start a conversation with someone you don't know, and it turned out to be a fruitful conversation. Maybe you received an introduction from a friend or a colleague that led to a career opportunity. Whatever it is, take the time to acknowledge your efforts and accomplishments. Celebrate small wins as much as big ones.

Identifying Areas for Further Growth and Development

Networking is a lifelong process of building and maintaining relationships. There is always room for further growth and development. Identify areas where you can improve and work on them. Maybe you need to focus on building a stronger personal brand, or maybe you need to improve your communication skills. Whatever it is, set goals and take action.

Creating an Action Plan for Ongoing Networking Success

To achieve your networking goals, you need to create an action plan. Start by setting specific and measurable goals. Identify the strategies you will use to achieve these goals. Determine the resources and tools you will need and create a timeline. Break down your goals into smaller, achievable steps, and track your progress. Make adjustments as needed and celebrate your successes along the way.

Committing to Lifelong Learning and Self-Improvement

Networking requires continuous learning and self-improvement. Keep yourself updated on the latest trends and changes in your industry or field. Attend workshops, seminars, and conferences. Read books and articles. Learn from your mistakes and successes, and from others' experiences. Commit yourself to lifelong learning and self-improvement.

Embracing the Power of Personal and Professional Relationships

Lastly, networking is not just about achieving your goals; it is also about building meaningful relationships. Embrace the power of personal and professional relationships. Nurture these relationships, be a good listener, show empathy, give back, and help others achieve their goals. Keep in mind that networking is a two-way street, and your efforts will not go unnoticed.

Applying Networking Skills beyond Traditional Settings

Remember, networking is not limited to traditional settings such as business events and conferences. Apply your networking skills in your everyday life, such as at social gatherings, volunteer events, or in your community. The more you practice, the more natural it will become.

Continuing to Expand and Cultivate Your Network

Lastly, continue to expand and cultivate your network. Seek out new opportunities, meet new people, and build new relationships. Stay in touch with your existing contacts and continue to add value to these relationships. Your network is a valuable asset that can help you achieve your goals and support you throughout your life.

In conclusion, Networking is an art that requires effort, time, and patience. By following the tips and strategies discussed in this book, you can become a master networker and achieve your personal and professional goals. Remember to be authentic, genuine, and respectful, and always look for ways to build long-lasting, meaningful relationships.

Final Thoughts

So there you have it, the art of networking. It's not just about exchanging business cards or adding people on LinkedIn. It's about building genuine relationships with people who share your interests, passions, and values.

Networking can be nerve-wracking, especially if you're introverted like me. But remember, everyone has something to offer, and everyone wants to feel heard and appreciated. So don't be afraid to start a conversation, ask questions and listen attentively.

It may take time to see the results of your networking efforts, but eventually, you'll start to see opportunities arise that you never imagined possible. Whether it's finding a mentor, landing a dream job, or even starting your own business – networking can open doors that you never knew existed.

So don't wait any longer to start building your network. Attend events, join groups, and connect online – but always do so with sincerity and authenticity. The relationships you build could change your life for the better in ways you never thought possible.

Thank you for taking the time to read this book on the art of networking. I hope it has inspired you to take action and start building meaningful relationships in both your personal and professional life. Good luck!

ABOUT THE AUTHOR

Ray Goodwin

Ray Goodwin, is the author behind this series of captivating books on Business Development and self improvement, and has left an indelible mark on the field. He was born and raised in the bustling city of London, where he developed a strong work ethic and an insatiable curiosity about the inner workings of successful businesses. Throughout his illustrious career, Ray leveraged his extensive knowledge and experience to help numerous companies flourish and prosper.

His keen insights and innovative strategies has earned him recognition, driving him to share his expertise with others. Ray believes in the power of sharing knowledge to elevate businesses and empower aspiring entrepreneurs.

Ray's dedication to his craft is evident in the numerous books he has authored on business development and self improvement. His writing style seamlessly blends practical advice, thought-provoking concepts, and real-life case studies, making his books invaluable resources for business professionals and novices alike. His ability to distill complex concepts into accessible language has greatly impacted the lives and careers of countless individuals.

Now retired from the corporate world, Ray and his beloved wife have settled in the idyllic English countryside. Surrounded by the beauty of nature, Ray finds inspiration for his writing and indulges in his hobbies.

Ray Goodwin's books continue to serve as enduring guides for those seeking success in the business world. With a wealth of experience and a deep understanding of the inner workings of businesses, Ray's work remains a testament to his passion for sharing knowledge and helping others flourish.